The Pilgrim's Way

Become the Master of Your Spiritual Adventure

by Ixchel Tucker

Copyright © 2018 by Ixchel Tucker

Throughout history our stories are how man has passed down our wisdom, experiences and learning. They can be fun and enlightening, sad and heart-rending. In this book, I have included many of my personal stories and experiences for this purpose, so that they may inspire you or show you what I've learned.

FREE BONUS BOOK

Get *Magic Comes Alive in Mexico*, by Ixchel Tucker.

This short story tells of my life-changing adventure of quitting my job and driving my car and trailer all the way to central Mexico. Without knowing anyone there, I had no idea what I was doing or what to expect. That's when the best adventures happen!

Go to my website and sign up for my email list for your free book:

www.adventurequestsintl.com

The Cover Photo

Like other sacred sites, the image of this little church on Lake Bled called to me. I knew nothing about it, just that I wanted it for the cover of my book. It felt like the perfect image for pilgrimage and sacred travel.

It doesn't surprise me to learn that this island in Slovenia has been known as a sacred site dedicated to **_Živa,_** the Slavic goddess of life and fertility *(much like **Ix'Chel** is to the Mayan people.)*

The island is a pilgrimage site. At the apex is a small church dedicated to Mary. It has a special wishing bell.

I haven't been there, but this is how I am generally drawn to new destinations. I just know in my soul that I should go. Lake Bled is one of those places I've now added to my list, as I continue to adventure and explore the sacred sites of the world.

Photo credit: Ales Krivec @dreamypixel, Pixabay.com

Discover Lake Bled, in the Julian Alps of Slovenia:

https://www.bledoscope.com/bled-island/

Table of Contents

Chapter 1

The Spiritual Adventure

"Twenty years from now you will be more disappointed by the things you didn't do than by the ones you did do. So throw off the bowlines. Sail away from the safe harbor. Catch the trade winds in your sails. Explore. Dream. Discover."

Mark Twain

You are about to embark on a sacred journey. Each life carries its elements of the journey or quest. In this book you will learn to bring more intention to your calling for adventure, more clarity to your own journey and gain greater insights as you evolve and bring through more of your own true self.

Every day is sacred, every moment, every space. So, what are we talking about in mastering our own sacred journey?

First of all, I will define what I mean by these terms:

Mastery

Mastery means to practice something until you become the best you can be.

In this course, I refer to your Mastery as the practice of bringing conscious awareness and intention to your acts. Everyone can learn ideas and often spout them out as their ideals of how one should live. It is easy finding 'teachers' who want to teach their way, their perspective or their ideas.

Mastery is a step above teaching or ideas. Mastery is taking the ideas we've learned, ciphering out those we believe make the most sense for us, and living from them. Mastery is taking each experience and integrating it into who and what we are, to find our own truth. Mastery is a practice, not an idea.

Being a 'master' means practicing this integrated approach in your life. You can be a master at anything you set you mind to. You can be a master at yoga, meditation, karate, your work, or even with your play. You can master love, being love and radiating love. When you integrate it all, you can master being your true self.

This book will help you find this truth within you. It is designed to lead you to become master of yourself and your own truth as you discover your own way to quest, journey or pilgrimage in the world.

Spiritual Adventure

The term Spiritual Adventure is combining the spiritual and sacred with the adventure. It is taking spiritual concepts out into the world, where they can be experienced.

This is where we get out of our comfort zone and we are faced with the grit of life. We will meet other cultures, we will visit sacred space, we will 'call or invoke' Divine help and guidance ... and we will be transformed.

As you read this book, I encourage you to get out and use it in the world. Find and create opportunities for yourself to put the steps into practice. **Make pilgrimage a part of your life as you explore sacred places and experience your own journeys, both large and small.**

Begin seeing the world with new eyes and you will learn to find the sacred all around you. Some sacred sites are well-known; others are not. Sacred places can also be anywhere you feel at peace and feel a connection with the Divine. Often they are in nature. Sacred space is connected with churches or shrines, ancient structures such as pyramids or lost cities. Sometimes they are special places you discover on your own such as a favorite hilltop or grove of trees.

You will learn to connect with elements of nature, with gods and goddesses, with saints, archetypes of ancient cultures and more.

The practices in this book will guide you to seek out and find sacred encounters and transformational experiences. In the process, you will open to a deeper experience of you that is waiting to be born.

Chapter 2

What kind of Experience do you want to have?

"The purpose of a pilgrimage is about setting aside a long period of time in which the only focus is to be the matters of the soul. Many believe a pilgrimage is about going away but it isn't; it is about coming home. Those who choose to go on pilgrimage have already ventured away from themselves; and now set out in a longing to journey back to who they are.

Many a time we believe we must go away from all that is familiar if we are to focus on our inner well-being because we feel it is the only way to escape all that drains and distracts us, allowing us to turn inward and tend to what ails us. Yet we do not need to go to the edges of the earth to learn who we are, only the edges of ourself."

— L.M. Browning, Seasons of Contemplation: A Book of Midnight Meditations

Quest, Pilgrimage, Ceremonies and Rites of Passage

The steps in this book can be universally applied to experiences such as Vision Quests, Spiritual Pilgrimage, and transformational retreats. However, there are some differences in these various types of experiences that may help you decide which is a fit for you.

Vision Quest

A Vision Quest is an indigenous ceremony that has been offered by Native American cultures as a 'coming of age' or 'rite of passage' ritual for young adults (traditionally male). This type of ceremony typically involves the person going out alone, in nature, or "on the mountain", and stay for three to four days, while fasting, and "calling for a vision."

Most of us haven't grown up with a 'rite of passage' such as this and later in life we may feel called to this type of ceremony. This day and age there are many ways that Vision Quests are offered, and they are generally open now to both men and women of all ages. You may find Native Americans and others who have trained and apprenticed in their tradition that still follow the old rituals. In these ceremonies, it is common to ritually prepare for a full year prior to questing. The preparations involve making prayer ties and infusing your prayers and intentions into a chain of prayers that will hold the boundary of your physical space throughout your quest. This prep time adds a richness and depth to the experience.

There are also New Age or more contemporary methods of questing. These may take pieces of the old traditions and weave them with other training or practices that help with your transformational experience. Feel into which type of ceremony you are called to and which leader(s) you feel you can trust as your guide.

Pilgrimage

Pilgrimages are integral to many spiritual traditions. They are a common religious practice that may even be expected or required by some faiths. Even if you are not religious or part of a specific faith, a pilgrimage can deepen your connection to the Divine.

Common elements of pilgrimage

- A commitment to your path from the day you walk your first step. This is an internal commitment between you and God/Spirit or your Higher Self. There is often no one telling you where to go or stopping you from straying from the path, and some detours may be perfect for your pilgrimage. Yet most people have their own internal rule in place that if they leave the path, they then start back in the same place they left, not further on. It is understood that if you 'cheat' or take shortcuts you are only 'cheating' yourself.

- Your commitment keeps you going each day. Some days will be very difficult and you will have to push yourself to keep going. You may ask yourself why do you keep going, and you may want to quit. But the deeper commitment, the one you make to yourself, is what often gets you through those challenging times.

- Most traditional pilgrimages are made by walking from start to end. They involve strain on your body, pain and blisters on your feet, carrying your belongings in a backpack and other physical discomforts.

- The experience is often deepened by daily devotion with prayers and other rituals. You may walk alone and in meditative contemplation.

- You arrive at a sacred destination. The sense of completion when you cross that threshold at the end gives you a deep accomplishment that can never be experienced any other way than by walking it.

Ceremonies for Transformation

Your pilgrimage or journey may incorporate various ceremonies, from initiations to completions and everything in between. These ceremonies can mark certain points along the way and help anchor in your experience.

You may have opportunities to participate in some different types of ceremony while on your adventure, so I will explain some of the ceremonies I'm familiar with or have participated in.

This is, by no means, a comprehensive book about ceremony. It's always good to ask your own questions and do research. If you are being invited or expected (as part of the group) to participate in a ceremony, it's a good idea to find out what you can about the specific ceremony you are attending. I recommend that you also get a feel for the person who is leading it and make sure you feel comfortable with them.

If you've never done a certain ceremony it can be a bit intimidating. This guide will help you to understand what these ceremonies are about and what you're getting yourself into before you say yes. Remember, the choice is always yours to make.

Sweat Lodge *(or Temazcal in Mesoamerica)*

The sweat lodge is a purification ceremony that has been used in indigenous cultures since ancient times. In North America the lodge is traditionally made of tree limbs crossing over each other to create a domed frame. The frame is then covered with layers of blankets to keep the heat in. In other areas, such as Mesoamerica, the lodge may be made of adobe or some other solid material.

Typically, rocks are then heated in a fire and brought into the center of the lodge by a fire tender. Water pourers will add water to the rocks to create steam and the medicine man (or woman) leading the sweat will add herbs, say prayers and sing medicine songs. There are four (or more) "doors", with the door opened in between and more hot rocks brought in.

Each person offers their prayers to Spirit as well. The sweat lodge purifies and cleanses you on all levels: physical, emotional, mental and spiritual.

This type of ceremony was traditionally used when a warrior would go off to fight or at the beginning of a longer ceremony, such as a vision quest. Travelers and traders coming back to the community would also partake in a sweat lodge prior to returning to the village as a way of clearing out the energies they had picked up from other tribes.

When done well, a sweat lodge can be a powerful experience for letting go. You can come out of it feeling like you're light as a feather.

Things to be aware of:

The sweat lodge is dark, hot and confined. If you have issues with being in dark, tight spaces, you might want to consider whether you are ready to push through your fears or sit it out. If you have health issues, especially heart problems, the intensity of the heat may be too much for you.

Generally a sweat lodge is only opened between doors. That is when you can leave, if needed. Talk to the person running the sweat before going in. Ask them what their policy is about leaving the sweat. Sometimes the leader will work with you, others will expect you to power through.

Medicine Ceremony *(with hallucinogenic plants such as peyote or ayahuasca)*

Native Americans and other indigenous tribes have used hallucinogenic plants to gain spiritual insights and reach higher realms of conscious. This practice dates back thousands of years and evidence of the ceremonies has been found by archaeologists around the world. The medicine ceremony has been a sacred practice, led by a shaman.

You may find these types of ceremony available as you travel. Peyote ceremonies are common in Mexico. Ayahuasca ceremonies are easily found in South America and are even practiced legally in the United States through the Santo Daime Church.

Some organized tours will include a medicine ceremony as an option, when it's available. My recommendation is that you find out more about the plants or ceremonies you are interested in, if possible. Find out how experienced the shaman (or person administering the ceremony) is.

Precautions

As a precaution, be aware that people have died in some types of ceremonies such as sweat lodges, peyote, ayuhuasca, and others (generally involving something physically straining on the body or hallucinogenic plants). The medicine man leading the first sweat lodge I attended had a man die of a heart attack in one of his lodges. The worst public case was in 2009 in Sedona, Ariziona when several participants were rushed to the hospital and two people died after not being allowed to leave the sweat lodge. The leader of the retreat was prosecuted, but that is little solace to those who died.

This isn't to say you should avoid these type of ceremonies. For me it's important to get to know the ceremonialist and what they are like. If I don't feel good about the person leading the ceremony I may back out or at least make sure I can leave when I want to. The warning here is to be aware of what you're getting into, and if and when you can get out.

Chapter 3

Finding and Experiencing Sacred Sites

"Only those who risk going too far can possibly find out how far they can go." — T.S Eliot

Sacred Sites, Thin Places, Ley Lines

Sacred Sites are places that hold a strong energy signature. They are places where you feel and sense there is something more than what you see. They have been described as *"thin places"*, a place where the veil between heaven and earth is thin and we are able to feel a stronger connection to the Divine.

Since ancient times man has known of these places and traveled to them to pray and perform ritual. Temples and pyramids have been built on power places, designed with sacred geometry and precision, to harness this powerful energy.

Sacred sites long forgotten are being rediscovered at an amazing rate.

Around the world there are headlines of new sites being found. With the use of satellite imagery there are more temples and pyramids being discovered all the time. We are in a time of awakening and emergence of the Divine Feminine and this correlates to uncovering of sites for goddesses as well, bringing new understanding of the role that women played in our history.

We're remembering the ancient knowledge and wisdom that was hidden, buried and forgotten. Though the written records may be lost and the people long gone, the wisdom is within each of us. Going to these sacred places helps open the portals within us, opening to our deeper knowing that has been buried inside.

"As above so below. As within, so without."

The outside world and the inside world are one. Everything in they Universe also exists within you. When you visit sacred places you can use this understanding to align the outer experience and the sacred energy you feel into your body and soul. Let what is in you come alive.

Sacred Buildings and Structures

Buildings and structures are the most obvious of sacred sites. Cathedrals, temples, churches, mosques, and synagogues are easy to find. These places were built with sacred intention and have been visited over time by devotees who come to pray, perform rituals and bring in the spirit of God or the Divine. Even if the land was nothing special to begin with, the sacred intention of the visitors builds an energy.

Often the buildings were also constructed with sacred intention. For example, when building the Chartes Cathedral in France the workers would begin their day with meditation and prayer. If they were unable to get into a heart space for the day they would go home and not work that day. The entire construction was completed from that heart space. Imagine what it feels like to be in a cathedral that was built in the energy of love.

Ancient structures such as pyramids, temples, dolmens, and hedges were generally built in alignment with the energy of the earth. Many are also aligned with each other to form energy triangles or power lines. In Mesoamerica the pyramids were built to reflect the sacred Mayan and Aztec calendars and rituals of ascending the pyramid were part of their spiritual path to enlightenment. The precise shape of pyramids, whether in Egypt, Asia or the Americas, has been shown to amplify the energy of the earth.

Additionally, as the Roman Catholic Church expanded and enforced their way of worship on others they built their cathedrals and churches on top of the temples of the Druids in Europe, the Incas in South America, the Aztecs in Mesoamerica, and others. They knew that these sacred sites were aligned with the ley lines and took advantage of their energetic placement.

Sacred Land

In nature you can find rocks, mountains, rivers, waterfalls, wells, forests, groves, and even pilgrimage routes that have been held as sacred by people for centuries. A few examples are:

- Ayers Rock, Australia

- Devils Tower, Wyoming, USA

- San Francisco Peaks, Arizona, USA

- Wao Kele o Puna forest, Hawaii, USA

- Ganges River, India

- Chalice Well, Glastonbury, England

- Camino de Santiago, Spain

These sacred places in nature have subtle and different meanings to the people that were originally there. Some places are known for their stories and may have ties to the creation myths of the indigenous cultures.

Energy Vortexes

Energy vortexes are a unique energy center found on the land where the energy swirls around, similar to a whirlwind or whirlpool. They are charged with a strong electromagnetic energy. They have been reported as conducive to healing, meditation and self-exploration.

What to expect at a Sacred Site

The powerful energy of a sacred site can be felt in many ways. You may feel a tingling in your hands or the hair standing up on your arms.

You may have a feeling of discomfort or unease at one site, while feeling happy or euphoric at another. Each person is different and each site will be different. You will feel differently each time you revisit a site.

Sacred sites will amplify the energy within you. What this means is that whatever is happening within you gets stronger and more intense. So, if you are feeling good, you will feel better. If you are feeling down or depressed, you may feel worse. If you have an open mind and connect to the spirits of the site, you can have an insightful and profound experience. Yet, negative thoughts and beliefs can also intensify. This is true in your everyday life, your thoughts manifest your reality. You will just find this amped up at sacred sites.

Spiritual and New Age people flock to Sedona, Arizona; Mount Shasta, California; Byron Bay, Australia and other places known for having strong energy centers. Their strong attraction draws many people to move there. What they don't realize is that these places can be difficult for people to live in. Not only will it push you in your inner growth, but relationships can be very challenging when living in such places. This isn't good or bad, it's just intense.

Truly, all of God's land is sacred. If you have a special place that feels sacred to you, go there often, connect in whatever way feels right for you.

Trust what you know in your gut

I've had so many experiences where I've been warned against visiting a place (by some well-meaning friend or acquaintance), yet, following my own intuition and going anyway I've had a very good experience.

One that really sticks in my mind was Pompeii. It was the last day of an organized pilgrimage that took us to Medjugorje and Assisi. After a day in Rome, we had a free day to spend as we chose. I found out that Pompeii was only three hours away and I wanted to go ... my soul wanted to go!

Yet, there were people in the group warning me that it wasn't a good place. In the history of Pompeii, everyone is buried and dies from the volcanic eruption. They told me when they had visited it had a very heavy and dark energy.

I went anyway. I love ancient cities, old places long forgotten by time. And this one was really calling to me.

I had an amazing experience. I took my time exploring the city and loved everything I saw. It was sad to see how the people had died. Yet, it was incredible to see how they had lived. Many buildings were still intact. There were tiles on the floors and frescoes on the walls. The city was beautiful.

At the end of the day I wandered down a side road to a building called "The House of

Mystery". The feeling of love and connection I had felt all day got even stronger. My heart felt like it was expanding, almost out of my chest. I knew - somewhere within me I just knew - that I had, had a past life there. I once had lived in that home. I walked around the house and checked out all the rooms. I could see myself as a child running through the halls.

I am so glad I went, not listening to the advice of my friends. What was true for me was different than what was true for them. It may be that their ideas of the place and their focus on death clouded over the experience when they went, or it could just be that this place wasn't for them. That's not important. What was important was that I chose what was right for me.

How to connect to the energy

Now that you understand that your own energy, thoughts and beliefs will be magnified, you may realize that clearing out negative thoughts and beliefs will help you have a more positive experience. The best way to do that is with meditation and intention.

As you are entering a sacred space or site, begin with a prayer or invocation. Ask the sacred energies of the place to connect with you and ask their permission for your entry.

If possible, find a quiet space and do a meditation to help clear out your energy. (Or you may want to do this in the morning, before arriving at the site.) Focus on breathing in the energy of the Divine and breathing out all energy, thoughts and beliefs that are not in alignment with your true self. Take the time you need to come into your heart center.

Tuning into the energy of the sacred site

Each site has a unique energy that is different for each person experiencing it. The best way for you to know what it is for you is to tune into the energy and ask what it holds for you.

- You may get the impulse to sing or dance.

- Or you might feel that playing drums or rattles is right for you.

- You might feel compelled to sit somewhere and go deeper into meditation.

- Or to touch the rocks or stones.

- The energy may stir your emotions. It can make you smile or cry. Whatever you feel, don't stop it. Allow yourself to feel your feelings.

As you connect, follow your intuition and continue asking what this place has in store for you.

Remember not to be attached to the outcome. Let go of expectations. There will be some places you visit where you have no distinct feeling of connection. Yet others will open your heart. Even when you aren't feeling anything, there is still something happening on a more subtle level, behind the scenes.

Challenge yourself. Be aware of your fears and push your limits, but only as far as you are ready to go. Find the balance of stretching yourself, while not going too far, too fast.

Ask for and expect support from others, such as your leaders or guides. Let your guides help you feel safe and supported on your journey. When you feel safe in being held and supported you can stretch a little further, knowing someone has your back.

Most of all, embrace the adventure. When your spirit calls to you to experience more of life, follow it's guidance. The more you open and connect to your divinity, the more you open the channels for you intuition and inner truth to flow.

"Whatever's good for your Soul, do that."

Your soul withers and dies when you ignore its needs. Open to the possibilities and discover a new world, a new you.

On a sacred site trip to France in 2012 I found myself pondering the power of the sites that I was visiting and how to 'work' with their energy. We were with a guide who was quick to point out where the energy centers were, but did nothing to help us understand them.

It was about our third day on the journey and there I was, in Saintes Marie de la Mer, standing in the chapel, in front of a painting of Jesus, where he had his hand over his heart.

As I gazed up at the painting I thought to myself that I didn't need some Divine Revelation. All I really wanted was to be able to bring through as much love as Jesus did in his lifetime. I wanted to live my life from that place of pure love. I wanted to do as Jesus, to help others know how truly loved and special they are, to bring people closer to their own divinity.

I stood there, right on the energy center where the ley lines crossed, and focused my intention in that way. I focused on feeling the energy, bringing it into me, so that I could find more of my own divinity and use it in that way. I felt good. It was simple and it was enough.

My experience in France reminded me that the way we connect with the power of sacred sites is different for each of us, and different each time and with each place we visit. There is no right or wrong way. Whether we feel the energy or not, it affects us and we get what we need and what we are ready for and open to receive in that moment.

MASTERY PRACTICE

Visit a sacred site near you. Before you go, learn what you can about the site. Tune into it. Ask the question, "what is there for me?"

If a negative feeling comes up, follow it. See where it takes you. Negative feelings or experiences are often an opportunity to clear away an energy that you wouldn't otherwise know was in you. From a Shamanic perspective, this can be your biggest teaching.

If you feel resistance, can you step through it? Are you ready to let go of what hasn't served you?

On the other hand, positive feelings may arise. You might feel wonderful! Explore what the message is for you. If you are ready, open your energy even more. Bring in as much of your truth as you are able to hold.

Chapter 4

What is your journey about?

"We run toward our challenges. If we love it, something is going to happen. We begin to have a different relationship with our fears, our frictions, our challenges that is exciting … we see the opportunity to open and grow."

People can travel to sacred sites and not get much out of it. Many sacred sites tour groups offer a full itinerary of sites to visit, but with little support into what sacred travel is. To get the most of your experience, sacred travel can be looked at as a Quest or Pilgrimage with steps or thresholds along the way. The journey can be embarked on with meaning and purpose.

The Steps of a Transformational Pilgrimage or Journey

Step 1. The Call to Adventure

We feel a call to go, the call of our wild nature inside, longing for something more. Our Spirit awakens to this calling. Where do we go? What will we do? What calls to us?

Step 2. Commitment

When you commit to your journey things start shifting. You may start having profound dreams or have strange and fun synchronicities start showing up in your life. This is a time that your resistance can also play a strong hand. Your spirit is saying YES, but your ego and its worries can take hold and make it a bumpy ride.

Step 3. Preparation

Preparation encompasses the physical, mental and spiritual aspects of your journey. From listening to our intuition to journaling about our dreams, there are many ways Spirit will begin to prepare us for our journey. The moment you commit to any transformational growth or experience, your preparation begins. During this time you may face various challenges and resistance, bringing up doubts about what you're doing and making you wonder if you should go on the trip.

Step 4. How to Travel in a Sacred Way

What is different in the way we travel when on Pilgrimage or Spiritual Adventure? It is travel with purpose and intention. Rather than stubbornly clinging to ideas and expectations, open yourself new experiences and perspectives. We can often feel more of Spirit in us when we walk in silence, even closing our eyes to pick up on other senses and feelings.

When you travel with a serendipitous spirit you open yourself to the magic that happens along the way.

Step 5. The Journey

Your journey is a HERO'S JOURNEY. You will be letting go of some aspects of self, while discovering and embracing parts of yourself you had buried, forgotten or pushed aside. It can be frightening, enlightening, exciting and fun. Often your best experiences come where least expected.

Step 6. Homecoming

Integrating the new aspects of you can take time. Coming home from a life-changing experience can feel very strange. You re-enter the mundane world of tasks and schedules, work and family. How do you hold on to the gifts you've received? How do you walk in the world differently?

Chapter 5
The Call to Adventure

The two worst strategic mistakes to make are acting prematurely and letting an opportunity slip; to avoid this, the warrior treats each situation as if it were unique and never resorts to formulae, recipes or other people's opinions.

-Paul Coelho

STEP 1. The Call to Adventure

How do you recognize your call to adventure?

We know we want more out of life when we are feeling restless, when we hear of other people's adventures and wish it were us. We feel the call when we see movies, pictures or videos of places that draw our attention and awaken our wanderlust. There is a wild nature deep within that longs to be fulfilled. Sometimes our desire is so strong we can barely think of anything else.

You'll feel it in your bones.

I remember several years ago, I was attending a concert performed by a Peruvian Elder. He was playing ancient water pipes, drums and flutes, while flapping condor feathers. The primal energy stirred something in me. Along with the concert they had a slide show of the mountain village he was from. Just seeing the pictures brought me to tears. My heart longed to go there.

This feeling surfaced again and again, whenever I heard of friends going on a trip or saw something advertised, I would feel the call to adventure. Our soul has its ways of providing opportunities to fulfill our dreams. When the dreams come from the soul-level they don't just die or go away. Even when denied, our soul finds its way.

So it happened that synchronicities lined up and one day I got a phone call, out of the blue, from a man that had a company leading sacred site tours. He hired me as his web master. Working in the office, behind the computer wasn't where I wanted to be, but at least it was closer. Every time I put together an itinerary I longed to be part of his tours. The strongest calling I felt was for a trip to Southern France, which I finally was able to join. It was an incredible experience that still calls me back for more.

Begin with your calling

Where is it that calls to you? For your soul truth to speak to you, you've got to get past the mental chatter. Dare to dream! If you could go anywhere you wanted, right now, if money, time and other commitments were no object, where would you go?

Take a few minutes to meditate with the question. Allow your answers to come to you.

Meditation -
What/Where is Calling You?

Begin by finding a quiet space where you won't be disturbed.

Turn off your phone and quiet any potential interruptions. If you live with others, ask them not to disturb you. Find somewhere you can sit or lie and get into a comfortable position.

Close your eyes and breathe into your center. As you breathe in, focus on the energy from the heavens coming down into the top of your head and down throughout your body, filling every cell with Divine energy. As you breathe out, let go of all energy that is not yours. Let go of any stress or tension or thoughts of your day.

Continue breathing in and out and allowing the energy from above to fill you, while letting go of tension and stress.

Now focus your attention below you. Imagine your energy stretching down, into the earth, deep into the center of the earth. Imagine roots extending from your body and into the earth. Breathe in the energy from the earth, up into your body and coming up through your legs and into every cell of your body. Feel it as it mixes with the energies from above.

On your out breath continue to let go of thoughts and energies that are not yours. Let go of any stress and tension. Turn over your problems and concerns to the earth where they can be transformed.

Now bring your attention to the center of your being. Ask the question: "Who am I?" Breathe into the deeper truth of yourself. Allow a picture to form of your true Divine nature.

Ask yourself, "Who am I in this moment?" "What is my soul calling me to? In the journey of life, where am I being pulled to go?"

The answer may immediately come to you. If not, just allow yourself time to see, hear, feel or sense an answer. It may not be clear, even as you continue your meditation. Often answers can come to us later in the day, or in our dreams, or even days later when an insight hits us.

Continue to ask and allow your journey to awaken in you. Even if a destination isn't clear, you may see, hear, sense or feel yourself in a scene. Explore the scene. What are you doing? Why are you here?

Take as much time as you like in this meditation. Feel deeply into your truth. Notice how good it feels to be with yourself, your true self.

When you feel complete, give thanks and gratitude for this time together with your Divine Self.

Coming back into your body, take deep breaths, breathing yourself back in. Begin to notice the room around you. Feel your body.

Take a deep breath as you feel your feet and legs. Wiggle your toes.

Take another deep breath in and feel your

torso and breath deeply into your lungs. Begin moving your arms and stretching.

On the third breath, breath into your head and move it back and forth. Breath into your third eye, in the center of your forehead. Stretch your arms over your head.

When you are ready, open your eyes.

After the meditation, you may want to write down what you experienced and any insights that came to you. Continue to add to it anything that comes into your awareness in the next day or two.

Learn to listen to your intuition and follow the messages you receive. Your life will open up and change in wondrous ways.

Be a Seeker

Spirit speaks to us when we are open to the question. Your path will flesh itself out as you ask yourself the questions:

The Who? What? When? Where? How? Why?

Let the Divine take care of the "how"

With spiritual adventures it's best to turn most of the "how" over to the Divine. The best part of working with the Universe or God as a partner is that when we are clear on what we want we can turn the how over to God. Very creative and magical solutions can show up, sometimes faster than you can imagine. We just have to be open and pay attention.

"Who" will you go with?

Will you go alone or with a group? Do you want to go on an organized tour, one that you don't have to be concerned about details or itineraries? Or do you prefer to plan it out yourself?

FINDING YOUR MASTERY

As you step into **practicing our own mastery**, it can be very helpful to have a guide or teacher who can lead the way. The wisdom of a good teacher can take you further than you might have pushed yourself and offer you insights that you might not have seen for yourself.

Find the right support

Whether you are going solo or with a guide or leader, you should consider what type of support you will have and need. Support is something we don't well understand in our modern culture. Yet people used to live in communities and tribes where helping each other out was intrinsic to their way of life.

These days we are living in independent and me-focused times; we often think we can do everything for ourselves. Even with our spiritual teachers and leaders, their focus is often more about their teaching than it is about support of the person following it. These two things combined leave us going into ceremony, sweat lodge, workshops and other experiences often lacking the support and guidance we need.

Finding What Support Meant to Me

I had never even considered what support really meant until I was in my forties. It's not that I wouldn't have appreciated some support, but I had little choice. I had raised my kids as a single mother, with no help from their father and minimal help from family. I learned to be independent and alone. I got used to doing everything for myself.

Then I got an opportunity to participate in a Vision Quest ceremony. This is an indigenous ceremony where you go out on the mountain alone and fast for three to four days, asking for a vision. I was so excited! This is something I knew deep down that I wanted to do.

Our vision quest involved a full year of preparation and we were expected to bring someone to support us. Our intercessor (or leader) explained that for my Quest I was expected to bring one or two "right-hand" supporters. Our "right-hands" would help keep an eye on us while we were questing. They'd tune into our needs, keep the sacred fire burning, and even dream for us.

I had a hard time finding anyone to be that "right-hand" for me. I asked some friends, but still couldn't find anyone that could afford the time (a week away, camping out in the desert or mountains) and personal expense, as well as the overall willingness to support me in that way.

Fortunately, things turned out well and I was supported by an entire group of people I hardly knew, those who were part of our questing community. These new friends all choose to come to quest for the purpose of supporting those of us who were questing.

This experience opened me to a whole new way of seeing things. It taught me to look at my friendships, as well as my spiritual leaders, differently. I've always been the kind of person who likes to give and to do things for others. This taught me that in addition to giving, it's important to receive as well. Since then, I've developed deeper friendships with people who will help me out when I need it and I've learned to ask for help more often. Six years later I quested again and this time I easily found friends that were happy to show up and support me. I've supported my friends during their quests, as well.

When it comes to a spiritual quest or journey support is very important. We need support with not just our physical needs, but also with emotional, mental and spiritual aspects of the quest. We are opening to some deep, inner growth and we need to feel safe. People have trusted their leaders at times with disastrous consequences. As mentioned previously, people have died in a sweat lodge and others during a medicine plant ceremony (such as peyote or ayahuasca). While I encourage everyone to take risks, taking unnecessary risks is just foolish.

If you don't already have a good support system in your life, it's a good time to start developing one. We should all have friends we can count on to help us in times of need.

What type of support will you need? Who will provide it for you? With good support in place, you can feel better about the physical and spiritual risks you are getting ready to take.

Traveling Solo or with a Group

Traveling Solo

If you are going somewhere on your own, where you don't have anyone else to watch out for your safety, you may not be able to go as deep into your experience. This isn't to say you won't have a deep and meaningful experience. Being alone can be many times better than being with the wrong people! It just means you won't have anyone else to fall back on, so you'll have to be your own watchdog.

Some people feel better traveling solo, without trying to follow along with anyone else's ideas or agendas. This can be especially true if you're highly empathic and pick up on other people's feelings and energy. Or perhaps you like the serendipity of going where your heart calls you, in each moment; not making compromises to fit someone else's desires.

If your intention is to go deep, you might want to consider asking someone you trust if they can energetically watch over you (from home) during your journey. It's best if they know how to work in realms of spirit and understand how to support you.

Whoever you choose, you can let them know when and where you are going and what you plan to do. People skilled in Shamanic or Native practices often understand what this type of support is. Energy healers, ministers and even good friends can support you in this way.

It's always good to let someone know where you are and what you're doing, even if they are simply your emergency contacts and loved ones. These days you may also take your cell phone along and hopefully will have cell reception. *However, keep in mind that it's for emergencies. If you are going into a sacred experience, you won't want to be checking your phone, social media or email the entire time.*

Traveling with a companion or group of friends

This is a good idea if you are inclined to create your own adventure. The experience of going with someone can enhance the journey and also provide some direct mutual support.

If you are making this a deep spiritual journey, be sure you are going with people who are part of that. You should make plans together and understand mutual and personal intentions for the trip. Going with people you have a good connection with can make the difference between having the transformational journey you are hoping for or coming home disappointed and thrown off of your quest.

Going with a tour leader or formal group

My recommendation for anyone going with a group on a spiritual journey, or even into ceremony, ritual, massage, or energy work is that you feel into your intuition about the leader or therapist. Some leaders and guides have apprenticed or trained to be conscious of the energy they hold for you, others are only trained in the technique or other aspects of what they are doing. And in the New Age spiritual communities there are often people who are not so much trained as that they get their calling from Spirit and go for it. This doesn't mean they aren't excellent at what they do, or that they don't intuitively know how to support and hold space for you. I am just suggesting that you use your discretion to find what is best for you.

Hearing the Voice of your Intuition

Intuition is a tricky thing. When do we push forward? When to we pull back?

Each situation calls for us to be aware of the voice inside. And the situation can change at a moment's notice.

MASTERY PRACTICE

This is a book about you finding your mastery. **Remember that your intuitive hunches are much more important here than anything logical.** You are developing a better sense of that through every journey you take and everything you do. It is better to walk away, even push or shove yourself out the door, than to regret not listening to your intuition.

Sometimes We Have to Make our own Door

My first sweat lodge was with a Native Elder and Medicine Man that told us to let him know if we needed the door open. He said we should yell it out if we weren't heard.

He encouraged us to take care of ourselves, even to go so far as to make our own door out the side if we needed to.

*This is much better than the person who tells me I have to stick it out and power through. **A good shaman will push you to your limits, but only you can decide how much to push yourself.***

There's a story of *"Jonathan Livingston Seagull"* that was published in 1970. It told of a young seagull that thought life should be more than just scouring the beach for food. He had dreams of flying higher than any seagull had ever flown. The other seagulls ridiculed him and told him it couldn't be done. He ended up expelled from the community. However, he kept pushing himself and learning all he could about flying. He found new teachers that taught him even more. Eventually he brought his higher learning and his peaceful way of living back to his flock.

Like Jonathan Livingston Seagull, we will never know our abilities if **we don't reach beyond our perceived limits.** It's good to push our limits and strive for something we haven't done before. The key is to know when to push and when to pull back, hopefully before we've gone too far. Sometimes you'll know it in that little voice inside that says *"this is enough"*. Listen to it.

My intuition was telling me "NO," but I wasn't listening

I learned this lesson the hard way one day. I have always had a fear of deep water that seems to be connected to past lives of drowning. I'm not much of a swimmer. I love being around water, I just don't always feel comfortable in it. It's one of those fears that's deeper than logic.

I used to go soaking at a mineral pool in Ashland, Oregon and enjoyed it immensely. I had a friend that asked if I'd ever done Shitzu, a water massage technique. I told him I hadn't and he offered to do it with me. He held me and moved my body through the water in a way that felt wonderfully safe and sweet, like being in the womb. None of my water fears came up.

So years later, when a friend offered to do a similar technique called Janzu, I thought it would be good. But, the movements were very different. Instead of relaxing, I found the motion difficult on my body and very uncomfortable. I started feeling sick and had to stop her. I quickly left the pool and physically vomited by the side. I didn't know if I'd ever try it again.

A few more years went by and I ran into another lady that did this technique. This was in Mexico and she didn't speak good English, so I tried to explain to her the two different experiences I'd had. She seemed to understand and I got the feeling that she could do something more like my first experience. I liked her and I liked her energy.

Perhaps a week later I had a vivid dream where I saw someone carrying a large fish that was stretched across their forearm. The next day I ran into this same Mexican lady walking home from a local festival. She was carrying a plastic dolphin on her arm in the very same fashion. I felt that it was a message for me that I should get a session from her, so I scheduled one. It felt right.

However, on the scheduled day, I hesitated to leave the house. When I did, I got there late. But, she was behind schedule and I had to wait while she finished another session. As I watched her moving her client through the pool I felt myself tighten up. I didn't want to be moved around like that. My mind started thinking of ways I could get out of doing the session. But my reasoning mind told me that I'd already scheduled to do this and I should get over my fears. So, I went ahead with the session.

When she was ready for me I told her I needed it to be much more gentle than what she did with the other client. She seemed to understand. Then we got in the water and she started moving me around, pulling and stretching me in different ways, and moving my body through the water. I wanted to trust her, but my soul was freaking out. I felt like I was being tortured and my soul didn't want to stick around. I could feel it wanting to leave, almost like it was screaming. I started reaching out energetically to the people I know that could help me on a soul-level and asking them to help keep me safe. Yet, eventually I could feel my soul and body split, as my soul let go. I'd never felt anything like this in my life. I felt a strange disconnect, as I was still aware of the soul/body split, but I had no idea what to do to get my soul back into my body.

After the session the lady sat me down on the side of the pool and I just sat there without moving for quite a while. She had no idea what had happened and I didn't have the language to tell her. When I told her I had a bad experience, her response was that I was holding on too tight. She didn't have the training to understand the soul and past life issues I was going through. I had been holding on tightly, to try to keep my soul in my body! With her as my guide, I truly wasn't safe. It was no fault on her part, she did what she was trained to do, she simply didn't know.

I finally got up and had to walk back to where I could take a collectivo (mini-bus) to go home. I knew that dirt and walking were good for grounding. But walking didn't seem to help at all. I bought a snack, food is also good for grounding, but again, I felt no better.

I got home and started calling my friends. One friend said she had a big intuitive hit to call me that morning and warn me (though she wasn't sure about what), but she wasn't sure enough about her intuition and she hadn't. I called another trusted friend who does powerful energy work. He was one that I had reached out to when my soul was panicking. He did some work on me and yet I still didn't feel connected. Finally, I remembered a friend that does shamanic work. He did a shamanic journey over the phone with me and got me back in my body. But it was a really scary experience, and one that taught me that even with a massage (or water massage) you have to be careful of who you work with.

Most of all, it taught me to trust the intuition that was telling me to get out of there. I'd felt it that morning, before leaving, and felt it even stronger when I was watching her with the other client. But I let my reason win over my intuitive hunches.

I've also realized that when I'm not sure whether fear or intuition is guiding me, it's OK to rule on the side of safety. Without some of my previous training in leading ceremony and understanding of my soul I probably wouldn't have even known what had happened or who to call for help. I was lucky to know people that understood when I told them about it, friends who supported me and that knew how to work on a soul level to help.

MASTERY PRACTICE

As in my story, learning to listen to and heed your intuition takes practice. This is when hindsight is good, think back on the times in your life that you "just knew in your gut" that you should or shouldn't do something, but you did the opposite. It can be wise to pay attention to the voice of reason, but the magic happens when you listen to your heart and soul. Start to pay more attention to that small voice within.

Your decision about who to travel with is important to your journey. Feel into what is right for you. Find leaders, teachers and friends who take the time to listen and see you, those who encourage you to be the best you can be.

What? When? Where?

This is the time to go back to your calling and the urges you feel. Is there a place or places that you long to go? Is there a historical or mythical story you feel connected to and want to know what that connection is about? Is there a mythical god or goddess you have a connection with? Or a saint or hero? What land calls you? Are you drawn to pyramids, temples, or sacred mountains?

Some people choose to follow a journey they read about, like an adventure to Avalon in England or discovering Mary Magdalene in France. Others visit the Greek or Roman temples and connect to the gods and goddesses. The options are endless. You can find tours to almost any of these destinations.

To get started, you can research areas around where you live. You can find sacred cathedrals and buildings, special mountains and more. Learn what you can. Take a small trip and see what it's like to connect in your own sacred way.

Why?

What is your Sacred Purpose for this journey? To discover this you must delve into the inner calling itself. What message is your soul trying to get across to you?

Sacred Travel is Travel with Intention

Intention is very different from expectation. Intention is a commitment to self, a commitment to discover more of your inner true-self. With intention your journey will guide you through a swirling mist of illusion and story and into the deeper truth behind the smoking mirrors.

The difference between Expectation and Intention

With expectations we often miss the magic. Expectation can get us into a more mental state that says something like "if we are at this Sacred Site something should happen." Or expectation may have us focused on some outward appearance of comfort, need, or image. With these expectations we can miss the true beauty hiding under the surface.

However, expectation isn't all bad. If you are feeling that good things and miracles can't happen in your life, try to turn over that doubt by reminding yourself that God or the Universe wants you to live your greatest joy. Then, rather than expecting the worst, let yourself expect the Universe to deliver magical gifts and they will come to you from all directions.

Intention is different. Intentions can be:

"I intend to open to anything the Universe would like me to realize at this time."

"I intend to go on this journey with an open heart and mind."

"I ask for clarity and understanding of what this place means to me on a soul level."

More specific intentions for a journey might be:

"I intend to let go of things that are blocking me from discovering my true path."

"I intend to discover more of who I am."

"I intend to know my life purpose and mission."

"I intend to feel more connected to spirit and my intuition."

"I intend to open my heart to receive love

Your intention may be outward or inward. Your preparation for your journey will help you develop an intention that fits your journey at this time. Each quest you take may have a different purpose or meaning to you and will likely be very relevant to what is going on in your life at the time. Every experience, even going to the same place, will be different every time you go.

It will be unique to you, to the time in your life, to where you are in your growth and understanding, and many other factors as well.

Chapter 6
Your Commitment

"When you find your path, you must not be afraid. You need to have sufficient courage to make mistakes. Disappointment, defeat, and despair are the tools God uses to show us the way."

Paul Coelho, Brida (1990)

Step 2. Commitment

This part of the journey is marked by a shift that will take place when you say **"YES, I'm going!"** Your commitment can take the form of making a deposit or payment toward your trip. Or it can come later, as you are packing for your trip. Sometimes you don't fully experience your commitment until you are stepping off the airplane or arriving at your destination. Once you've made your commitment, resistance can show up and it's good to be aware of how it can affect you.

MASTERY PRACTICE

Begin developing a view of your life from your soul's perspective. Rather than thinking "What do I want?", ask yourself **"What does my soul want?"** When your soul needs are met, it ignites an aliveness in you that is felt throughout your being and in everything you do.

With practice, you will begin to discern between the times when it is your intuition is telling you "NO, this is not for you!" vs. times when you are hitting resistance and moving through it is your opportunity to embrace more of who you are.

When you commit to your journey, your soul knows it. Your soul is rejoicing that you listened to your inner calling and you are going on this journey!!

But the other parts of you, your ego, your habits and your personality may wake up and say "What the heck are you doing??" You may suddenly feel resistance and that you can't go on this pilgrimage or quest. Knowing what the journey is about will help you as you walk through any challenges that come up.

Resistance and Challenges

Now that you've made your commitment, people often experience resistance and challenges. Some ways you might see this play out are:

- Worry about the cost of the trip

- Feeling overly concerned about taking time off or what will happen while you're gone

- Something bad might happen that will make you question if you should go on the trip. I've seen people get costly traffic tickets, have a loved one go into the hospital, and other financial or life challenges show up right after they signed up OR in the week or so before leaving for the trip.

- You feel anxious, have strange dreams, or question various aspects of the trip.

- Somewhere along the way your are likely to hit your walls. These are your opportunities to look at your thoughts, ideas and beliefs that have limited your soul's expression. What do you choose to do?

Is this Resistance or Intuition?

Keep in mind that **resistance is a very normal part of all soul-level work.** As you work on your own mastery, you can use a few tools to help determine if what you are experiencing is resistance or perhaps intuitive insight (telling you not to go).

Take a moment in quiet contemplation or meditation and ask yourself why you choose to go on this trip/journey/retreat/quest?

- Feel into the initial feeling and calling

- What spoke to you? Why did you choose this journey?

- How do you feel about it now? What does your heart say?

- How would you feel if you didn't go? Would you feel like you missed out?

- If this challenge weren't there, would you go? For example, say that your entire trip was paid for you, how would you feel about going?

- Close your eyes. See yourself going on this trip. How does it feel?

- Now, with your eyes still closed, see yourself staying home. See the trip happening without you, the other participants going. How does this feel? Do you feel left out or like you missed your opportunity?

If it helps, journal about this experience. Take time with it. Rather than impulsively calling to cancel, take a few days to work with the energy and feelings you are going through.

Keep in mind that you can always go again, at a later date. **The Universe will always give you another chance to have the experience your soul craves. In fact, it won't go to sleep or stay quiet until you do.** However, there will never be this same set of circumstances, the same group of people, the same timing with who you are now and where you are at in your life.

How do you feel about this time and this opportunity?

On the other hand, **sometimes our intuition is waking up and telling us that there is something wrong** and this isn't the time/place/or group for us to go with.

Some clues that will help you know if this is the case are:

- You feel a persistent fear around the upcoming experience

- Every time you move towards the journey/experience some kind of block comes up

- You feel a foreboding or warning

- Perhaps you have angels or guides that you communicate with regularly telling you not to go. What is their message?

- Despite rational thought, you just feel this isn't right for you.

As you are developing your own inner guidance and mastery, it can also be helpful to check in with friends or spiritual or shamanic guides. You may find talking to the person leading the trip will help you sort through these feelings.

Another great way to get insight is to toss a coin. Say "heads I go, tails I cancel my plans". Whichever way it lands, how do you feel about the answer? Do you feel happy or sad? Relieved or upset? This will tell you what your true answer is. (Don't necessarily cancel your plans because you got tails. If you feel really upset that tails showed up, you know that your true answer is that you really want to go.)

One perspective is the more resistance you feel, the more it is telling you to go. The bigger your resistance, the bigger soul lesson for you to work through. While that has some merit, I haven't always found it to be true. Remember my story about the Janzu water massage?

As noted above, your intuition telling you NOT to go can get very loud and insistent. Sometimes it is right. My personal belief is while I will often move towards resistance and working my way through it, I have also learned to trust that if I feel I should quit/leave/or back off, I am better to err on the side of caution. **Mastery is all about finding these answers for yourself.**

As you're going through this, be gentle on yourself. Don't judge yourself or be down on yourself for canceling or backing out of something you truly don't feel is right for you. And don't let anyone else bully you into feeling like you're wrong. You are the only one that can decide what is right for you!

Moving Through my Resistance and Fear

I had heard of firewalking, but I never, ever thought of doing it myself. Firewalking is where they build a big bonfire and let it burn down to the coals. The coals are spread out in a rectangle about five feet long and three feet wide. You then walk barefoot across the coals.

I had never even really considered it. However, I was taking an apprenticeship course in Spiritual Ministry and we had an assignment to participate in different types of indigenous ceremonies. One of the options was firewalking. It was part of a list of things designed to push our limits such as ritual burial, vision quest and similar ceremonies.

Other students in our class talked about giving it a try. That didn't mean I needed to do it, but it prompted me to start looking into it more, researching about it online. I read that one of the big reasons people had for firewalking was that it broke through our preconceived thoughts and beliefs about our own limits and what we are capable of. That led me to realize that it was really just my fear holding me back.

I decided I wanted to do it. But then I had trouble finding a firewalk ceremony anywhere around where I lived, which at that time was in the California Bay Area. That seemed a bit strange, since it has such a big population base and there is always a lot going on there. Yet, I just couldn't find anything.

I finally found a firewalk ceremony and workshop that was being held in February on Vashon Island, Washington. I had some friends there and one of them said I could stay at her place, so I booked my trip.

When it came time for the firewalk we were all set in rows of chairs inside a big barn-style building. Before the actual firewalk we were led through several trust exercises and told about what to expect. The idea was to raise our vibration higher than the vibration of the hot coals. Then we wouldn't get burned. (I'm thinking, "Yep, that sounds good, BUT, are you sure about that?")

We all participated in the ritual of building the fire and each person had a piece of gasoline-soaked paper to bring their own light and flame to the fire. The wood was also soaked in fuel.

Then we went back inside. But, at this particular location we had a big picture window that looked right out at where the fire was burning. Throughout our workshop we were watching as the fire started burning and then dying again. The firetenders were working hard to get it to stay lit.

Finally, one of the firetenders came in and spoke with the workshop leader. The leader turned back to us as she explained that the wood was wet (it was in the Pacific Northwest in February and it had rained the day before) and they couldn't get the fire to go. She said they'd try once more, but if they couldn't get it going she wasn't throwing in the towel, but we might have to walk on just a tiny patch of coals.

I thought to myself what the choices were. Did I really want to walk on coals? I had come out of my way to be here, at a cost much higher because I had the flight and a rental car and other expenses, and I know that if I didn't do it then it would only get harder the next time. My investment and commitment was high.

However, there was another part of me that was scared. Every time I saw the fire blaze to life my fears had come up. Was I really doing this? I realized that my fears may have kept the fire from burning. It probably wasn't just me, there was a room full of people, but I knew I had my part to play.

I decided to put my intention on the fire burning well and that we could go forward with a very successful ceremony. As if by magic, it came to life.

I still hesitated and was one of the last to walk across the coals. I was sure my feet were burned. But what I thought might be a blister was gone the next day. I had faced my fears and pushed through to a new level of me!

Ironically, at the firewalk on Vashon Island I met a lady that was leading a firewalk in the Bay Area a month later. I went to it as well. But I think the Vashon Island thing was part of my soul's design, knowing that if it was less convenient and I had to go out of my way that my commitment would be bigger and that would help me face my fears.

Chapter 7
Preparing for Your Adventure

Step 3. Preparation

Once You've Made Your Commitment to the Trip, Your Journey has Already Begun.

The Shamanic Perspective

Your preparations build the energy for the experience you will have. The more time that goes into the preparation, the bigger the experience may be. As you connect more to your Spirit Guides, you are building relationships and they will show up more readily when you need them.

> Year-long preparations for Vision Quests are common, as are long apprenticeship programs. This time investment is not something we're used to in our society, where we are used to expecting an immediate reward.

The time of preparing for your trip is a part of the journey itself. In Native or Indigenous practices this is well recognized where the time in preparing for a spiritual quest can be as long as a year before the actual quest. The preparation may include prayers (and making prayer ties), deepening connections with ancestors and spirit guides, paying attention to your dream time, as well as having a spiritual mentor or guide to help navigate and integrate the experiences you have.

As you bring your own awareness and guidance to this time, you can do the same. Watch what comes up for you. The awareness you gain through this time will help clarify what your journey is about.

Spiritual Preparations

You will enhance your journey by consciously preparing for the trip in the following ways:

Pay attention to your Dream Time. What are your dreams telling you? Is there a common thread? In the morning, especially if you've had a powerful dream, take some time to journal about it and contemplate the insights that come to you.

Create a Ritual for your journey. Similar to the ritual of prayer ties, setting aside some special time to tune into your journey can bring further insights. A ritual can be as simple as lighting a candle and sitting quietly or placing elements on your altar. The ritual will connect you to the energy of the place or places you are traveling to.

Set up a Manifesting Altar. Perhaps your soul is calling you on a trip, but it's beyond what you feel you can afford. You dream of going somewhere, but there are obstacles that make it seem unreachable.

One way to attract your desires is to bring symbolic representations of what you want into the physical realm. Do this by creating an altar with various aspects to represent what you desire. You might use toys, stones, feathers and other symbolic objects. You can also include pictures and brochures of places you dream of going.

Years ago, before I came to Mexico to live, I did a ceremony and brought some things to my altar: a horse, an airplane, a toy of Dora the Explorer with her friend, Diego and her jaguar and a Volkswagon bus. Within a year I was living at a jungle retreat where I was helping guests. In my free time I'd visit pyramids and explore Mexico's magical towns. My partner had a Volkswagon bus. All the items on my altar had manifested in my life, in ways I never would have anticipated or expected.

Make a Vision Board. Another way to manifest your desires is to create a Vision Board where you make a collage of pictures of all the places you want to go.

Read about the Sacred Places where you will be traveling. Find stories about the gods/goddesses/saints related to places you will visit. Learn the history of the land. Developing connections with the beings and energy of the land beforehand will begin to open the channels of communication.

Amp up your Spiritual Practices – such as yoga or meditation. In whatever way you connect with Spirit or Source, as you do this more often you will open the door and magic will flow through.

Journaling. As you write about thoughts, ideas and insights your deeper knowing and wisdom begins to come through. You will find you are often picking up on answers to your own questions. Trust the information that comes to you. Write about anything that comes to you through your dreams, meditations, or other sacred practices.

Stay in a place of discovery and continue to ask questions. *A Quest is about questioning.* Who are you? Not just the you that is your personality, but the deeper you that is your soul. Why are you feeling called to go on this journey? What is calling to you?

Pay attention to synchronicities and messages, signs and meanings. This is a part of the magic and will continue throughout your journey. Let go of your agendas and ideas of how and what should happen and follow the path that opens up for you as the magic unfolds.

Practice Your Intuitive Skills. You've already been doing this, since it is your intuition that called you to the journey and your intuition is part of everything that you've done so far. Keep working on this and fine-tune your intuition so you will know and trust the messages you get. ***Remember, you are your own best master/teacher/guide.*** Listen and pay attention to insights all along the way.

Getting clarity on your Intention

Usc all this preparation to hone in and gain clarity of what your intention is and what your trip or journey is about. A theme is likely to present itself. For some it may be a journey to open the heart, others may learn about setting boundaries or speaking their truth. A journey can be about overcoming fears, connecting to others in spiritual community, or simply discovering a deeper sense of self. There is no one way or right way. Your experience is unique and special just for you.

Your preparation will help you open to the wonders and magic that Spirit has for you. You will discover a deeper clarity, and move through your adventures with grace and ease.

Other Preparations

By being prepared you will be more likely to enjoy your trip. You may be staying fairly close to home (you can have a wonderful journey in your own backyard) or you might be traveling halfway across the world or to a remote island in the Pacific.

The suggestions listed below can apply or be adapted to wherever you are going on your adventure or quest.

Physical Preparation

Consider where you are going and what type of preparation you might need. For example:

- If you are going to be walking or hiking a lot, you might want to get in better physical shape. In 2001 I went on a 4-day trek over the Inca Trail to Machu Picchu with my hiking club. For half a year we went on hikes 2-3 times a week, yet it still wasn't enough prep to keep me from getting altitude sickness (though it did help in other ways). You want your trip to be fun for you, so do what you can to be ready for the physical challenges and you won't have to miss out or stay behind.

- If you're going on a yoga retreat you might want to increase your practice.

- The same is true for meditation. Some trips or retreats involve long meditation sessions that can strain the body. It helps if you are used to sitting for long periods of time.

- For a Native-style quest (and some other similar experiences) there can be a long period of fasting. You can be more ready for this if you practice fasting for a day or more at a time beforehand.

You get the picture. When it comes to the physical challenges you'll face, take your overall health into consideration when deciding on the right trip for you. If you are unsure, you can also get a doctor's opinion before you go.

A good practice on a spiritual journey is that when you are hungry from fasting, tired from walking, too hot in a sweat lodge, or otherwise feeling pushed to your limits, this is the time to turn it over to God or Spirit. Ask him/her to take your hunger or tiredness. You may also use a mantra such as "I am getting stronger" or "I am getting through this with grace and ease."

Vaccinations and Health Precautions (especially for foreign travel)

Find out if there are any vaccinations required for the country or place you are visiting. If you are going with a group, they should inform you of what you will need. An internet search for travel requirements for the country you're visiting should let you know if there are any special requirements.

When traveling to Third World Countries, you should keep in mind that water might not be as clean and their standards for food preparation and storage are not what we're used to. Parasites and other diseases are more common. Some recommendations include:

- Drink only bottled water and use bottled water to brush your teeth.

- Eat cooked fruits and vegetables, unless you can be sure they are washed thoroughly. (You can buy or bring a vegetable wash from home if you are preparing any of your own food.)

- Don't eat at open markets, especially later in the day when meats have been sitting out all day. (I learned this first-hand when I ordered tacos late in the afternoon and it made me sick for weeks.)

- Bring along a treatment for food poisoning or bacteria so you'll have it at hand should you need it.

Logistics

Consider where you are traveling to and who you are traveling with. If you are going on an organized tour or trip, most of this will be taken care of for you. Things to consider:

Transportation – How will you arrive and depart? Where will you meet your group? If it's up to you to buy your plane ticket, be sure to get it enough in advance and be careful of arrival and departure times. Some cities have multiple airports, and bus or train stations. Be sure to note which terminal you need to be at and when. You might want to bring maps and chart out your itinerary.

Passports – Be sure that your passport is up-to-date and your expiration date is more than six months of when you will be traveling. TSA and most tour agencies require this. If you don't yet have a passport, apply for one as soon as possible. Don't put it off until the last minute. Passports can take up to three months to process (in the US).

VISA's – Research the countries you will visit and what their travel requirements are. Some countries automatically provide a VISA at the airport. Others must be purchased in advance, sometimes even before you leave the US. Some countries also require entrance and/or exit fees that must be paid in cash. Be sure to have the proper amount and currencies available when this is the case.

If extending your trip, such as taking in a few extra days to enjoy Paris, you will need to plan or organize the lodging and extra details around this. Some tour agencies help with these things, but keep in mind you will be on your own and plan accordingly.

If you're planning your own adventure, you will also need to plan your own lodging, food and transportation, of course, requiring more extensive research and preparation.

Guide Books. Unless the entire trip is planned for you, it can be helpful to take along a guide book. This gives you extra help when you're at your destination and a little more flexibility.

I like to plan for the major details, but also leave some room for going with what feels right once I'm there. With the guide book you can find out more of the options available and it makes it easier to make some of those decisions on the spot. My favorites are the Lonely Planet and the Hidden Travel series.

MASTERY PRACTICE

As you make plans and prepare an itinerary, think about how your energy works. On a trip like this, you are opening on some deep levels. All your energy centers are awakened and you are expanded and sensitive to the world around you. In this state, you can be overwhelmed when you find yourself in a busy city, with the world rushing by and people everywhere.

Because of this, I have found that it works best to plan busy, fun, touristy activities, especially when visiting busy cities, at the beginning of a trip, before getting into the deeper Spiritual journey. Also, if possible, build in a gentle way to get grounded back into your body and protect your energy before going back into a busy space and the 'real world'.

Packing

Packing depends on where you are going. It's good to get a list together in advance to make sure you don't forget anything important. If you're going with an organized group, ask them what they recommend you bring.

Things to remember:

- Passport and Visa (if required)

- Plane Tickets and other reservations

- Itinerary – take a printed copy with you and leave one back at home with your family or other contacts there. It's a good idea to let people at home know where you'll be and how to contact you.

- Anything special for the country or area you are visiting.

- For Sacred Ceremony you might want to (or be asked to) bring along ceremonial objects, such as a drum, rattle, staff or other items.

- Ceremonial clothing or something to wear for special occasions.

- Yoga mats, loose clothing, etc.

- Good walking or hiking shoes.

- Anything else that is unusual that would apply to your journey.

For up-to-date travel advisories for the country or countries you will be traveling to, visit: https://travel.state.gov/content/passports/en/alertswarnings.html

TSA also has Travel Tips and other information regarding Security Screenings: https://www.tsa.gov/travel/travel-tips

MASTERY PRACTICE

Remember to keep listening to your intuition and be aware of your surroundings (both physically and energetically) when you travel.

You can set the intention to put a protective barrier around you to keep you safe. I've also practiced the "Jedi mind tricks" like when Obi-Wan Kenobi said "these aren't the droids you're looking for." I've used this many times, such as when going through customs. When you use a mindset practice like this and develop it as a habit, you can travel happily and with minimal concern.

When it comes to intuition, keep in mind that it is perfectly acceptable to not get on a plane or not go on a trip at the last minute.

If there is something going on with political unrest or for any other reason (even just a big intuitive hit that you should not board the plane), listen to your guidance.

On September 11th, 2001 a lot of people learned this lesson. There were many stories of people who worked in the World Trade Towers but didn't go to work that day. Others missed their plane. Who's to say what powers were at work and guiding them to avoid the catastrophe?

A Fateful Day for our Nation

On that fateful day of September 11, 2001, I was traveling by bus. I was scheduled to go on my first pilgrimage, my flight was leaving on September 13th.

Early in the morning of Sept 11th I boarded a bus that took me from Medford, Oregon to the Bay Area, where I would catch my flight a two days later.

Right before boarding the bus I got a call from a friend to tell me about the bombing of the World Trade Center. As the bus traveled south the story unfolded. At our first stop, in Weed, California, we saw the news footage on a TV in the terminal. Our next stop was Sacramento, and by then they were talking about shutting down all areas of transportation, including bus stations. We made it to Vallejo where my kids picked me up and for several days all fights were canceled.

At that point I didn't know what was going to happen to our planned trip. Later I found out it was being rescheduled for a month later. But I was very happy not to be on a plane that day.

It's good not to hold on to our agendas too tightly. *Allow for delays. It may be intuition or Spirit, sometimes in the form of a traffic jam, airline delays or the authorities stepping in to help guide us to where we should be.*

Chapter 8

Travel in a Sacred Way

Step 4. Travel in a Sacred Way

Sacred Travel is travel with purpose and intention. Travel as a Seeker or a Pilgrim.

When we travel on Pilgrimage or Spiritual Adventure we are allowing for magic to happen. Be open to serendipitous experiences. **Every interaction along the way is a part of your journey (including delays and frustrations).**

Travel as a pilgrim, not as a tourist. Let go of expectations and have a bit of fun.

Set Your Intention

At the beginning of your journey you set your intention. Setting your intention will set the mood, transforming an ordinary trip into a life-altering experience. You can do this by stating out loud, writing it down or as a ritual or ceremony.

As you've prepared for your trip, your intention should have developed. If not, let it come to you in the moment. Allow it to come forth from your heart and your deepest desires.

Remember, intentions and expectations are not the same thing. An intention can be as simple as "I intend to connect to the sacred spirits of the places I am visiting". An expectation, on the other hand, is an attachment to the outcome, for example, expecting to have a vision of Mother Mary when you visit Lourdes. This kind of expectation can get in the way of the magic you are there to experience. Set your intentions and let go of your expectations.

Begin with an Invocation, Ceremony or Ritual.

You can create your own prayer, ritual or ceremony to begin each day or to set a tone when you are at an altar or sacred site. Or you may participate in specific rituals along your journey. Some spiritual leaders will incorporate ceremony into the tour. *The beauty of the ritual is that it opens the door to invite Spirit in, while at the same time quieting the busy and thinking mind, so that we are more open to messages from Spirit.*

Be Reverent. When you are visiting a sacred site, think of it as if you were visiting the home of God/Goddess or The Divine. Would you move about loudly, throwing trash and talking about your problems? Or would you enter in humility and silence? If you walk in reverence you are more likely to be treated with reverence and respect by the spirits or guardians who serve as caretakers of the land or sacred site.

Respect the Culture. Recently I read of a group of tourists who were visiting a sacred fountain in Rome, taking selfies as they waded into the water, as if it were a playground. The local people were appalled. They would never do this, it is their sacred water. This is just one example, of which there are many, where tourists abuse the attractions. Think and act with respect for the local cultures and traditions, rather than as a tourist that uses and abuses.

Walk in Silence. A nice way to tune into nature and the hidden realms is to walk in silence. This quiets the chatter enough that you can better hear and notice all that is around you, even the quiet voices of the spirits of the trees, the blowing of the wind and the water as it flows. You may connect to fairies, angels or other heavenly beings as you walk.

Spend Time Alone. Even when you travel with a group, take some alone time. Sit somewhere by yourself and contemplate or meditate. This is good to do at any sacred site or stop along the way. Take time in the morning before the activities of the day begin, or in evening hours when things slow down. *This is especially important if you are traveling with a spouse or partner, your child or even a close friend. If you want to have your own experience (growth and insights), you need to spend some time with yourself, away from the roles you have with others.*

Journaling. As you write about your experiences you take your alone time and your insights deeper. The writing helps to clarify your thoughts and makes them more concrete. Journaling allows more insights and messages to come through. This gives you something to go back to or share when you get home and your memories of your adventures will be even stronger. (*I know from experience that if I don't write them down soon after, the memories fade much more quickly.*)

A Pilgrim's Ten Commandments, *by Anonymous*

1. Thou shalt not expect to find things as thou hast them at home, for thou hast left home to find things different.

2. Thou shalt not take anything too seriously, for a care-free mind is a prerequisite for a pilgrimage.

3. Thou shalt not let other pilgrims get on thy nerves, for they art also children of God and their feelings also deserveth respect.

4. Thou shalt not be anxious, for they that are anxious gaineth no grace from

their anxiety, and few things are ever fatal.

5. Thou shalt remember that if God had intended us to stay in one place, he wouldst not have created us without roots.

6. Thou shalt at all times know where thy passport is, for a person without a passport is a person without a country.

7. When in the lands of the Bible, thou shalt be prepared to do somewhat as the locals do; and if in doubt thou shalt use thy God-given common sense.

8. Thou shalt not judge the people of a country by the one person who hast given thee grief.

9. Thou shalt remember to offer a "thank you" (and perchance a tip) to those who striveth to give good service.

10. Thou shalt remember that thou art a guest in others' lands, and they that treateth their host with respect shall likewise be treated as honoured guests.

Chapter 9
The Journey

"When we least expect it, life sets us a challenge to test our courage and willingness to change; at such a moment, there is no point in pretending that nothing has happened or in saying that we are not ready. The challenge will not wait. Life does not look back. A week is more than enough time for us to decide whether or not to accept our destiny."

Paul Coelho - The Devil and Miss Prym (2000)

Step 5. The Journey

Your journey is a **HERO'S OR HEROINE'S JOURNEY.** As with any journey of transformation, there are parts of yourself you are letting go of, lessons you are learning, and a new self emerging. Try not to cling too tightly as you face new experiences and your fears come up. Keep an inquiring spirit – ask yourself *'What is on the other side of this door?'* You may find unexpected treasures and gifts as you cross the threshold into something new.

Travel with a serendipitous spirit. Open yourself to the magic along the way.

Finding your Helpers

Who are the players in the story? There are players and roles in every hero's story. The hero has his sidekick, the wise sage or magician, warriors or protectors, and demons or antagonists. Be aware of how these archetypes show up on your journey. Sometimes they might be in the form of people, other times they may be in the form of a non-physical being or spirit guide. And still other times they may be within you, such as your inner demons or fears that are holding you back.

Understanding the role of each type of helper will help your grow through the experience.

The friend or sidekick. This person is with you through thick and thin. In The Lord of the Rings it was Sam. He would not leave Frodo's side. If you can find a good friend to be there with you on your journey, they are invaluable. They will listen to your challenges and watch your back. And most of all, you will know you are not alone. We often take turns playing this part for each other, both giving and receiving support.

The Wise Sage or Magician. This person may be a guide or shaman that is leading your group. If you've found a good fit, this person can give you insight into the spiritual journey you are moving through and how experiences you are going through are part of your soul's growth. You may also find this role filled by a spirit-being. I've felt the presence of Quetzalcoatl, Jesus, Mother Mary, Mary Magdalene, the Goddess Tonantzin and others on my various journeys. These relationships have gotten deeper along the way.

Your Warriors or Protectors. Feeling safe is important when you are going deep into your spiritual work and facing your fears. You want to feel your guides and leaders are taking care of you and have your best interests at heart. This can be as simple as providing comfortable lodging and food that you can eat. Or it can be more dramatic, where your physical safety is in question.

A protector may show up for you as your trip leaders or a friend. You may also have unseen protectors. At times when I've needed extra protection, I have called on my son, who was killed in Afghanistan in the army. He carries the spirit of a warrior. I know he's always with me and looks out for me, but when I need extra protection or vigilance I will call on him to make sure he's paying attention for me.

Again, in the Lord of the Rings, Frodo had a group of men, dwarves and elves protecting him while he was on his quest. This allowed him to focus on his journey with the ring. It helped give him the strength to stay in his heart and keep going. Think of how this may apply to your journey and who can watch out for you along the way.

The Demons and Antagonists. Every journey of growth has it's antagonists. They may show up as someone upsetting you. Or you may see the person as an enemy or foe.

The antagonist may also show up as a heavy energy, pushing against you or blocking your way. Often your greatest antagonist is an inner demon.

No matter how your demons show up, it's a good practice to ask yourself what is this showing you? What could this be mirroring for you? Is this other person illuminating a shadow or frightened part of you that is trying to stay hidden?

Even when your antagonist is in the form of another person, they can be externalizing a lesson or opportunity for you to heal, learn or grow.

MASTERY PRACTICE

You may again experience resistance, feeling like giving up or that something you are doing just isn't worth it. Remember back to the tools for understanding and working with resistance that were discussed in the

---

commitment phase of the trip. You may experience the same resistance or you may be going through something else entirely. This is another time to bring your awareness to the situation and learn what you can from it.

Should you power your way through or pull back? If you need guidance, this is the time your wise sage or elder can help you sort out what is going on.

Enhance the Magic of the Journey

As you travel on this mystical path, you are now in the heart of your journey. This is the phase of crossing the threshold into something new.

Crossing the Threshold

You are crossing over a threshold and into an unknown realm. You can enhance this feeling by walking through an actual doorway or portal. Notice these places along the way, where you feel you are walking into something new. How do you feel as you move into this space? What are you ready to let go of? What are you stepping into?

Be Aware of Synchronicities

Sometimes you meet someone along the way, or a stranger says "Hi" and it leads you in a whole new direction. Or you have a question you've been pondering and someone starts talking to you, giving you a new perspective or an answer to what was challenging you. Synchronicities show up in many forms, from a book falling off the shelf to a phone call you weren't expecting. When you pay attention to these sychronicities the magic comes alive.

I just had a fun synchronicity while writing the section on antagonists for this book. I was on a bus in Mexico and I wasn't paying attention to the movie they were playing, but when I looked up I realized it was Beauty and the Beast, the age-old fairy tale of taming the beast and finding he was a prince all along.

I experienced another one when I was writing the last chapter, the one about coming home. I was looking for ways to express the challenges we face when returning home. I was finishing reading a book, The Last of the Donkey Pilgrims. As he was returning home he beautifully expressed this phase of the journey (which I've included in that section).

For me, the synchronicities are always fun. They show me the magic is at work!

Follow Your Intuition

Intuition has been mentioned time and again throughout this book – because it's crucial to your experience. **Your intuition is your guide to your Soul's Journey**. Learn to tune in to its subtle messages. If it tells you to turn left rather than right, or follow a certain path or road, follow along and see where it goes. Sometimes your gut will warn you to stay away from something that doesn't feel right. Pay attention. Your soul will guide you to the experience that brings you to your highest potential. Let it take you along and see where you go.

It is much easier to follow synchronicities and intuitive guidance when you are traveling by yourself, at your own pace and with a loose itinerary. But even on a group trip you will find many places where you will be using these tools. Your intuition is like an instrument that you are continually tuning until you find just the right tone. Keep practicing and tuning in all along the way.

Make Offerings to the Spirits of the Place

When you offer a gift to the spirits you are inviting them into your life. Consider how it feels to be welcomed and invited in by friends or how good it feels to be given a gift. Offer gifts to Spirit and open yourself to the gifts you will receive in return.

Listen With All Your Senses

Listen with the ears that don't hear. See with eyes that don't see. Tune in to everything around you. Feel the breeze. Notice the birds and animals. What insights and messages do they have for you?

During the journey it's a good time to practice psychic tools like telepathic communication. When you hear the phone ring, ask yourself who is calling before you pick it up. You will get better and better at knowing who it is. There are many ways to practice this as you go. Get creative and tune into more of your psychic powers.

Let Your Truth Emerge

All along your journey you are changing and integrating. At times this will be dramatic and obvious. But at the same time so much is happening in the unseen realms and on other levels that you won't even realize it as it happens. Even when you aren't aware of it, you are transforming and becoming more of who you are. You are allowing in more of your Divine Self.

If you are traveling with a group, it's nice to share your experiences. This helps anchor them in. Talk about what's coming up for you. Process your feelings and listen to others. You might bounce things off each other and discover insights from each other's experience. My favorite way to do this is in a daily talking circle. Talking circles are a Native American practice where you pass a talking stick around the circle and as each person takes the stick it is their turn to talk. Everyone has a turn to share whatever is in their heart, with no cross-talk or giving feedback. As you speak from your heart, more of your truth is revealed.

Your pilgrimage or journey doesn't have to have a specific meaning and it doesn't have to make sense to your thinking mind. It might be something that is more felt than understood. Allow for whatever is true to you and accept that it is perfect, designed for what you need right now.

As Your Journey Comes to the End

Ending your journey or experience with a closing ceremony can also help to bring it all together. In ceremony you can invite in all the new aspects of you that have been awakened.

You can solidify some of this by journaling.

Answer the questions:

- Who am I now?

- What new aspect or awareness of me have I seen through this experience?

- What do I want to take home with me and remember?

- How will I integrate this new me into my life? How will I keep it alive?

You have just awakened a new precious part of you. Think of it like a newborn fairy, small and frail, and you are holding it in your hands. It will take some time for it to gain strength and for it to open its wings and fly. You will need to remember he/she is there. You will need to nourish this new you so that he/she can grow. Encourage your new self to fly. See the new you in the glory of radiating your light and shining in the magnificence of your being.

This is important. Without nourishment your new self will wither and hide back into the darkness, where he/she will have to be coaxed out once again.

Bringing conscious awareness to your newly transformed self helps you hold the new being that has awakened.

Chapter 10
Homecoming

"A man travels the world over in search of what he needs and returns home to find it."
Irish poet, George Moore

Step 6. The Homecoming

Integrating the new aspects of you can take time. Coming home from a life-changing experience can feel very strange. You re-enter the mundane world of tasks and schedules, work and family. How do you hold on to the gifts you've received? How do you walk in the world differently?

In his book, **The Last of the Donkey Pilgrims**, Kevin O'Hara talks of his homecoming and the challenges he faced:

> *"Here I am, twenty miles from Rattigan's, and despite all that might await me there, there's a part of me that wants this journey to linger on. Once I step foot into that pub, I'm afraid my house of cards will topple and I'll be left to face my own familiar self again. For eight months I've been blessed by this journey God has provided me. But now I face the unenviable task of returning home, where I might forget the valuable lessons I've learned on these roads."*

This is our challenge. How do we remember the valuable lessons? How do we stay true to our new self?

Coming back to your life can be the most difficult part of your journey. Your family, your friends and your job have defined you in certain roles and these expectations of others can pull you back to who you were. This can be a difficult time, when your habits can feel like heavy gravity that keeps you stuck in the past and you forget the new-self that has been born.

It can be depressing as you try to find balance again, remembering the free and beautiful self you discovered. Where did he/she go? How do you hold on to him/her?

You may find that your life doesn't quite fit you the way it used to and you might realize something needs to change. Perhaps a job or relationship needs to end. This is actually quite common as you awaken to your deeper truths. Those parts of you that settled for a life that was less than your deepest desires are now feeling more out of whack.

So, in fits and starts, you struggle to let go of the pieces that don't fit as you strive to bring in more of your truth.

This can be difficult to do, especially if big changes are called for. But this culling and emerging is required of you, by your true self, if you are to live the life of your destiny. It is a part of the mastery of being. And like all mastery, it demands your dedication.

Tools that will help with your integration:

1. **Awareness** – just being aware that these feelings are a normal part of the process will help you a lot in finding your way through it.

2. **Meditation** – Use a daily meditation that reconnects you to the true-self that you've discovered. This is the most powerful way to stay connected to that deep well within you.

3. **Ritual** – Create a new ritual or adapt one you used in the preparation phase to

anchor in and stay connected to your newly expanded self.

4. **Altar** – Add items to your altar that symbolize your journey and help you stay connected to the places you've been and experiences you had. You might add photos or a small statue or item of jewelry that you picked up on along the way.

5. **Journaling and Remembering** – Pull out your journal from the journey and read or share your experiences. You might add more insights to what you've already written as you explore the feelings you've had after coming back home. Create a scrap book. Keep the memories alive. They will fuel you with the energy to bring your experiences more fully into your life.

6. **Stay with the Questions** – Ask yourself questions like "how do I bring this new

awareness of me into my life?" Let Spirit guide your answers.

7. **Keep working on your relationships with the Spirit Guides and others that you met through your journey.** For example, after a pilgrimage to Assissi, Italy I felt a deep connection to Saint Francis. When I returned to San Francisco, California I researched and found that the National Shrine of Saint Francis was there. I often visit this sacred place in the city to reconnect to the energies of Saint Francis that opened up on my previous trip.

8. **Plan more Sacred Adventures.** You can keep going on sacred adventures and make them part of your regular life. They can be anything from a local day trip to a month-long pilgrimage. Find what works for you and keep the energy moving.

As you settle into being home and old habits surface, consider using a technique for changing your habits. There are many available. You could try using NLP (Neuro Linguistic Programming) or other brain retraining techniques to keep yourself from falling back into a rut or habitual way of being that is old and no longer fits your awakened self.

For all its challenges, the homecoming is where the rubber truly meets the road. This is when we discover if we have really been changed, or if we are just a creature of habit, returned to the comforts of home.

Chapter 11
Final Notes

"Your mind will answer most questions if you learn to relax and wait for the answer."

\- William S. Burroughs

You truly are your own best Master or Guide.

As you put into practice what has been taught in this book keep asking the questions. There is no one that knows what is right for you like you do. Others can help, but your knowing and truth come from within. Trust yourself. Trust in what you hear.

Keep practicing your mastery. Use you intuition.

Bring it All Together

These days there are many adaptations to the concepts of questing and pilgrimage. You may create or participate in a pilgrimage that doesn't involve walking a set path, but still involves intentional travel to a spiritual destination. A Quest doesn't have to be the traditional Vision Quest. In medieval times knights were often sent out on a quest, such as the quest for the Holy Grail.

Your Spiritual Travels will take many forms and be unique to you. If you travel with intention and visit sacred and ancient sites, you are bound to be transformed by the experience.

Continue to use this book as a toolbox or guide to bring in the elements that are important to you.

"The biggest fear is that we don't do it. You can always put obstacles in the way. We'll never do it if we keep thinking of reasons to put it off."

My hope is that this book will get you excited to get out there and have your own grand adventures!

Acknowledgements

There are so many people who've helped me in my life that to list them all would be exhaustive. However, I would like to thank those who helped me in relationship to this book.

I never would have envisioned this book if it weren't for all that I've learned from my teacher, Misa Hopkins. Misa has been my spiritual guide and the intercessor for my two Vision Quests. I have also taken several courses from her, including The Art of Ceremony, where she helped me understand what it truly means to work with the spirits on the other side and to hold ceremony for others. I've apprenticed with her to be able to hold Full Moon Women's Ceremonies that are from an ancient tradition and through that have learned what it means to hold space for myself, as well as for another human being. I have been so blessed to have her as a true teacher.

I also have great respect and gratitude for Ea Orgo, who took me under his wing and gave me the opportunity to work with him at his sacred retreat center in Mexico. He taught by example, with simple living from the heart. From him, I learned how to let go and not be attached to my mistakes or things gone wrong. I got to help set up and organize hundreds of sweat lodges and worked with retreat leaders and other guests. Most of all, I learned that my wisdom is within my heart and when I come from that space everything falls into place.

I'd like to thank Finbarr Ross for giving me the opportunity to work for his spiritual tour business: Celtic Mystical Journeys (they've since changed their name to Sacred Mystical Journeys). I not only had the delightful job of putting his itineraries onto his website, but I also got to write for his blog and provide customer service for those going on trips. It was a magical experience in so many ways.

I've had the opportunity to go on several sacred site tours and pilgrimages that have opened me in so many ways. In addition to quests and sacred travel that I've done on my own, I went with James Twyman to Bosnia and Italy, Finbarr Ross / Celtic Mystical Journeys to Southern France, and Illuminati Tours with Trudy Woodcock and Miguel Angel to Chiapas, Mexico.

When it comes to Pilgrimage, it has always spoken to me, but the pieces didn't quite fit together until I read "Waymarkers" by Mary DeJong. She gifted me with her book and it opened my eyes to see pilgrimage in a more transformative way. It helped me fit together all the pieces I had learned from shamanic work and questing with my passion for travel. We haven't yet met in person, but I'd recommend

Mary's pilgrimages and Rewilding Retreats to anyone.

Jennifer Blanchard Williams got me moving on the actual writing of the book. I give my heartfelt appreciation for all the support she gives to writers and potential writers. Her little program "Write and Publish Your Nonfiction eBook in 10 Days" got me from idea to action. (It took me much more that 10 days, but it sure helped to push-start me.)

Most importantly, my writing is nothing without good editing. I would like to thank those who helped me edit the book.

When the book was about two-thirds done, I found Amy Knickerbocker in the "Write and Publish Your Nonfiction eBook in 10 Days Facebook Group". We agreed to do a trade, to edit each other's books. I got the better end of that trade. She was so helpful, not just correcting my mistakes, but giving insight into what to add or take away, helping me out where things didn't flow or make sense. She pointed out that she's not my target audience, which probably gave her a more objective perspective that helped me find ways to express myself that were more clear to my readers.

After those changes, I added more content and stories, rearranged and took things out. It needed another eye on it. Donna Glory, my partner at Adventure Quests International, and Laurel Stuart did the final edits and gave some wonderful feedback. Thank you, ladies!

About the Author

Ixchel Tucker (born and known by her family as Shelley Tucker*) is a spiritual guide, mentor, teacher, ceremonialist and writer and author

As a freelance website and graphic designer, Ixchel has written numerous blog and magazine articles in the area of travel, sacred sites, sacred feminine practices, spiritual awakening, and personal transformation.

Ixchel has traveled around parts of Europe, the US, and Mexico. Her search for her true self has led her to explore her inner world through Vision Quests and indigenous ceremonies.

At the same time she developed a passion for sacred sites around the world, where she found an awakening between her outer world and inner knowing.

Her life is one of continual learning and evolving. She completed a year-long apprenticeship in leading Ceremonial Leadership and the Sacred Feminine and a deeper course in Spiritual Ministry. Additionally, she has worked for spiritual leaders including Neale Donald Walsch, James Twyman, Misa Hopkins, Finbarr Ross and others.

Ixchel has a gyspy-spirit that keeps her moving and exploring. Following an inner guidance she moved to Mexico in 2006 where she now lives part of the year, with the balance of her time in the California Bay Area, with her family. She has a love the outdoors, traveling, hiking, and dancing, connecting with people and meeting new friends.

Also by Ixchel Tucker

Ixchel is the author of:

The Pilgrim's Way - Become the Master of Your Spiritual Adventure

Magic Comes Alive in Mexico - An Adventure of Self Discovery.

Published as Shelley Tucker:

Forever 25: A Mother's Journey Through Grief (a memoir)

Ixchel is also author of numerous blog articles about Sacred Travel, Self Discovery, and Traveling in Mexico.

Her websites are:

adventurequestsintl.com

mexicosmagicdestinations.com

forever25.us

Remember to pick up your
FREE BONUS BOOK

This short story tells
of my life-changing
adventure of quitting
my job and driving
my car and trailer all
the way to central
Mexico. Without
knowing anyone
there, I had no idea
what I was doing or
what to expect. That's
when the best adventures happen!

Go to my website and sign up for my email list
for your free book:

www.adventurequestsintl.com

www.ingramcontent.com/pod-product-compliance
Lightning Source LLC
Chambersburg PA
CBHW071424150726
48000CB00001B/466